CW00642807

Wine Spectator's

CHAMPAGNE

Wine Spectator's
CHAMPAGNE

M. Shanken
Communications, Inc.
New York

RUNNING PRESS
PHILADELPHIA · LONDON

Library of Congress Cataloging-in-Publication Number 99-70309
ISBN 0-7624-0654-2

M. Shanken Communications, Inc.
387 Park Avenue South
New York, NY 10016

This book may be ordered by mail from Running Press.
Please include $1.00 for postage and handling.
But try your bookstore first!

Running Press Book Publishers
125 South Twenty-second Street
Philadelphia, PA 19103-4399

Visit us on the web!
www.winespectator.com
www.runningpress.com

Preface

*C*hampagne is the classic symbol of celebration — at weddings, birthdays, and of course New Year's Eve.

At the core of this tiny book is a sophisticated collection of observations, memories, wisdom, and witticisms from devoted enthusiasts of this magical, bubbly wine.

We've also included information and advice about Champagne, mini-features celebrating Champagne in the movies, and classic Champagne posters of the Belle Epoque era from the *Wine Spectator* Collection.

I raise my glass of Champagne and wish you health, love, luck and success in the twenty-first century!

Cheers!

Marvin R. Shanken
Editor & Publisher
Wine Spectator

Champagne, inseparable
companion of joyous heavenly
events, crown of festivities and
special celebrations. Champagne, symbol of friendship,
toast of state banquets . . . ritual
that launches steamships and
airplanes! Remembrance of
rebirth, joyful tear of anniver-
sary, stamp of victory and
peace, holy dedication of love.

—GENEVIÈVE DÉVIGNES
French historian, as quoted in
Champagne *(1993)*
by William I. Kaufman

Come brothers, hurry,
I am drinking stars!

—DOM PÉRIGNON (1658–1715)
*French monk accredited
with discovering how
to make Champagne*

The effervescence of this
French wine reveals the
true brilliance of the
French people.

—VOLTAIRE (1694–1778)
French philosopher and writer

Champagne in the Movies

In *The Seven Year Itch* (1955), a married businessman's fidelity is tested when new neighbor Marilyn Monroe drops by with Champagne and potato chips. When he opens the bottle, the Champagne floods out; he uses his thumb to stop the flow, it gets stuck, and much hilarity ensues.

Once they're finally drinking the stuff, Marylyn discovers a new taste sensation: dipping her potato chip in the Champagne. "It's really crazy!" she declares.

. . . Champagne with
foaming whirls
As white as Cleopatra's
melted pearls.

— GEORGE GORDON
LORD BYRON (1788–1824)
British poet

A luxury good enriches our lives. . . . It's like going to the opera. Those three hours, for which you're willing to pay a great deal, are so much more intense than an ordinary three weeks. They heighten your reality.

—REMI KRUG
Directeur Général, Krug Champagne

The priest has just baptized
you a Christian with water,
and I baptize you a French-
man, darling child, with a
dewdrop of Champagne on
your lips.

—PAUL CLAUDEL (1868–1955)
French diplomat and writer

Where do the bubbles come from?

All wines result from fermentation—the process by which yeast turns sugar (in grape juice) into alcohol and carbon dioxide gas. Fermentation takes place in large vats, so the carbon dioxide escapes into the air. With still wines, that's the end of the story.

But for Champagne and other traditionally made sparkling

wines, there's another step in the process. When the regular fermentation is complete, a small amount of sugar and yeast is added, and the wine is then bottled and tightly capped. A second fermentation now takes place, and since the gas can't escape, it becomes part of the wine—in the form of those tiny, delightful, nose-tickling bubbles.

Whenever I drink
Champagne,
I either laugh or cry . . .
I get so emotional!
I love Champagne.

—TINA TURNER
American singer

CHAM

DELE

AGNE

BECK

REIMS

Champagne in the Movies

Ivan: Why do you take aspirin
with Champagne?
Alice: Oh, Champagne gives
me a headache.

—AL PACINO AND DYAN CANNON,
from the movie
Author! Author!, *1982*

Champagne is the only
wine that leaves a woman
beautiful after drinking it.

—MADAME DE POMPADOUR
(1721–1764)
Lover of Louis XV of France

How dry or sweet is this Champagne?

Here's what some of the confusing terms on Champagne labels mean:

Brut: very dry (occasionally you will see extra brut, which is the driest possible)

Extra Dry: fairly dry, but with a touch of sweetness

Sec or Dry: medium sweet

Demi Sec: quite sweet

Champagne in the Movies

There comes a time in every
woman's life when the
only thing that helps is
a glass of Champagne.

—KATHERINE "KITTY" MARLOWE
(played by Bette Davis), in the
movie *Old Acquaintance*, 1943

CHAMPAGNE

DELBECK
REIMS

The feeling of friendship is
like that of being comfortably
filled with roast beef; love
is like being enlivened
with Champagne.

—DR. SAMUEL JOHNSON
(1709–1784)
British writer and lexicographer

Meeting Franklin Roosevelt
was like opening your
first bottle of Champagne;
knowing him was
like drinking it.

— SIR WINSTON CHURCHILL
(1874–1965)
British politician and writer

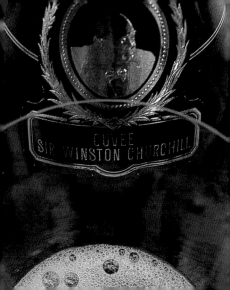

Champagne in the Movies

꽃

You've forgotten those June
nights at the Riviera . . .
the night I drank Champagne
from your slipper—
two quarts. It would have
been more but you were
wearing inner soles.

—GROUCHO MARX (1890–1977),
from the movie
At the Circus, 1939

Champagne for my true
friends. True pain for
my sham friends.

—ANONYMOUS

I drink it when I'm happy
and when I'm sad. Sometimes
I drink it when I'm alone.
When I have company, I
consider it obligatory. I trifle
with it if I'm not hungry and
drink it when I am. Otherwise
I never touch it—unless I'm
thirsty.

—MADAME LILY BOLLINGER
(1899–1976)
Champagne Bollinger

Disgorging

While Champagne ferments
inside the tightly corked bottle, a
sediment consisting of dead yeast
cells is left behind. After aging is
complete, the bottles are gradual-
ly turned upside down, so that the
sediment will collect on the cork.
The necks of the bottles are then
flash frozen; when quickly turned
upright, the corks fly out, carry-
ing a sludge of sediment with
them. The bottles are then freshly
recorked and readied for sale.

Many houses produced elaborately enamelled bottles in the Belle Epoque era (1890–1914), but only Perrier-Jouët uses such extrovert handiwork to commercialise Champagne today . . . with its flowers painted in pink, gold and green enamel, that is so evocative of the *joie de vivre* of the Belle Epoque.

—TOM STEVENSON
From Christie's World Encyclopedia of Champagne & Sparkling Wine *(1998)*

I drink Champagne at any
occasion—as an apéritif at
11 in the morning, after a
game of tennis or a swim in
the pool or sea. I enjoy drinking Champagne in all sorts
of places in Paris, whether
in a fancy restaurant or a
cozy bistro.

—CLAUDE TAITTINGER
Executive Owner,
Champagne Taittinger

I make wine for myself.

What I can't drink, I sell!

—VICTOR LANSON
Champagne Lanson

Champagne in the Movies

In Vincente Minelli's musical
Gigi (1958), a simple card
game between Gigi, a turn-
of-the-century Parisian girl
(Leslie Caron) on the cusp
of womanhood, and Gaston
(Louis Jourdan), the jaded
and wealthy family friend she
is being tutored to ensnare,
turns into a rollicking song-

and-dance number called
"The Night They Invented
Champagne," with Gigi's
grandmother (Hermione
Gingold) joining in. All
three are fueled by a bottle
of bubbly, which Gigi, in her
open-hearted naïveté, believes
was invented just for them!

My only regret in life is that
I did not drink more
Champagne.

—last words of
JOHN MAYNARD KEYNES
(1883–1946)
English economist

Three be the things
I shall never attain:
envy, content, and
sufficient Champagne.

— DOROTHY PARKER
(1893–1967)
American writer

Alas, I am dying
beyond my means.

—OSCAR WILDE, as he sipped
Champagne on his deathbed
Irish-born writer (1854–1900)

Vintage or Nonvintage?

Nonvintage Champagne is a blend of wines produced in different years. The winemaker tries to balance the blend so that the producer's "house style" stays consistent from year to year.

Occasionally, a single year's growing conditions are good enough to produce a fine, well-balanced wine that needs no assistance. In that case, a Champagne house "declares a vintage," and puts the year on the label.

It's a long time since
I drank Champagne.

—last words of **ANTON CHEKHOV**
(1860–1904)
Russian playwright

Champagne is the one thing
that gives me zest when
I feel tired.

— BRIGITTE BARDOT
French actress

Champagne! In victory,

one deserves it; in

defeat, one needs it.

—NAPOLEON (1769–1821)

RAHMS

Why do I drink

Champagne for breakfast?

Doesn't everyone?

—SIR NÖEL COWARD
(1899–1973)
*British actor, playwright,
and composer*

Tiny bubbles in the wine . . .
make me feel happy,
make me feel fine.

— DON HO
Hawaiian singer

Like the maturing of romance
into a deeper human attachment,
the making of Champagne is an
art that becomes engrained in
the lives of all who commit them-
selves. It must be conceived and
created from raw materials with
imagination, knowledge, inspira-
tion, hard work, and persistence.
It doesn't just happen. It is a life-
time work. It is a magnum opus.

—WILLIAM I. KAUFMAN (1922–1996)
*American writer and author of the
book* Champagne *(1973)*

Named after a Babylonian
king, Nebuchadnezzars
are the biggest bottles of
Champagne money can buy.
Standing just over 2½ feet
tall, Nebuchadnezzars hold
the equivalent of 20 regular
bottles of the top shelf nectar
of conviviality—enough to
fill the glasses of 160 of your
closest friends.

—FORTUNE MAGAZINE
October 27, 1997

According to *Christie's World Encyclopedia of Champagne & Sparkling Wine* (1998) by Tom Stevenson, there are 250 million bubbles in an average bottle of Champagne.

Champagne loves a deep chill.
It is what accentuates the
wine's crisp taste and tingle
and keeps the bubbles rising
to the top of the glass.

—SUZANNE HAMLIN
Food reporter, New York Times

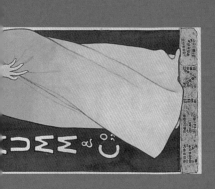

There are extra flavors in old Champagne that you just don't get when it's younger. People think after fifteen years you should get rid of it. But they're wrong. My Champagnes don't generally go flat, but I often enjoy them even when they do.

—RONALD WEISER
Michigan real estate executive and Champagne collector

Does Champagne need to be aged?

All Champagnes are ready to drink when you buy them. Nonvintage Champagnes spend a minimum of 15 months—and vintage Champagnes a minimum of three years—aging in the bottle before they are released for sale. This is plenty of time for the wine to develop its characteristic taste.

Vintage Champagnes, however, are special enough to develop even more complex and interesting flavors if properly cellared for a few years. But be careful! The bottles must be kept on their sides (so the corks stay damp), at a fairly cool temperature (55°F is best), or the wine may mature too quickly.

What is your hosts' purpose
in having a party? Surely not
for you to enjoy yourself; if
that were their sole purpose,
they'd have simply sent
Champagne and women over
to your place by taxi.

— P. J. O'ROURKE
American writer

O thrice accursed

Be a Champagne thirst,

When the price of beer's

all we've got.

—ANONYMOUS

If the aunt of the vicar has
never touched liquor,
watch out when she
finds the Champagne.

— RUDYARD KIPLING
(1865–1936)
British writer

Champagne in the Movies

The title character of Ernst Lubitsch's effervescent *Ninotchka* (1939) is an oh-so serious Soviet Communist apparatchik — played by Greta Garbo — who travels to Paris to recover some jewels. Cupid intervenes; the man with the jewels (Melvyn Douglas) falls for her, and spends the rest of the film trying to convert her to capitalist hedonism — including, of course, generous amounts of Champagne.

The bubbly wine makes Ninotchka the life of the party and thus leads to one of the most famous movie marketing slogans of all time: "Garbo laughs!"

I'm only a beer teetotaler,

not a Champagne teetotaler.

I hate beer.

GEORGE BERNARD SHAW
(1856–1950)
Irish-born playright

It is rumored that
Marilyn Monroe once
took a bath in 350
bottles of Champagne.

The most common wine in
Hollywood circles is Cristal
Champagne by Louis Roederer.
Whenever anyone does any-
thing good, they get a bottle.
A film opens, they send Cristal.
I don't think I've bought a
bottle of Cristal for myself
in five years.

— ROBERT SHAYE
Chairman, New Line Cinema

Champagne and Cuisine

Champagne is known as the drink of celebration. It is quite enjoyable as an apéritif and goes very well with appetizers. But it is also fine to drink at the table. Its crisp acidity makes a good match with many first courses that feature fish or shellfish, and it's good with lighter meat and poultry, too.

When you pour a flute full of
Champagne to enjoy, it's the
fine texture of the bubbles,
the depth and complexity
of flavor, and the lingering
finish that count. The best
Champagnes transcend mere
refreshment and celebration —
they are distinguished wines
that enhance the pleasures
of the table and can improve
with age.

Some take their gold
In minted mold,
And some in harps hereafter,
But give me mine
In bubbles fine
And keep the change
in laughter.

— OLIVER HERFORD
(1863–1935)
American writer and illustrator

In June of 1998, 500 bottles of 1907 Heidsieck Champagne were brought to the surface by divers exploring the *Joenkoeping*, a World War I Russian ship sunk by a torpedo from a German U-boat in 1916. Salvage organizers found the 91-year-old Champagne to be fresh and lively, apparently well-preserved by the darkness and 35°F temperature at the bottom of the Baltic coast of Finland.

It is my heartfelt wish

that it [Champagne]

spreads joy, peace,

and happiness.

—EMILE MOREAU
Quoted from Champagne *(1993)*
by William I. Kaufman

GRAND CRÉMANT IMPÉRIAL

CHAMPAGNE
De ROCHEGRÉ
EXTRA-QUALI

Posters of the Belle Epoque from the *Wine Spectator* Collection

Pierre Bonnard: p. 44: *France-Champagne*, 1891

Leonetto Cappiello:
   p. 39: *Champagne Delbeck*, 1902
   p. 45: *Pur Champagne/Damery Epernay*, 1902
   p. 124: *Champagne de Rochegre*, 1902

Abel Chalon: pp. 30–31: *Champagne Delbeck*, 1905

Georges Dola: p. 24: *La Chauve-Souris*, 1904

Alphonse Mucha:
   pp. 8–9: *Moët & Chandon/Champagne White Star*, 1899
   pp. 78–79: *Champagne Ruinart*, 1896

Maurice Realier-Dumas: pp. 92–93: *Champagne Jules Mumm & Co.*, 1895

Photography

Archive Photos: pp. 69, 74, 111
Archive Photos/Fotos International: p. 29
Archive Photos/London Daily Express:
  p. 80
J. L. Bulcao: pp. 40, 43, 53, 54, 56, 85,
  101, Endpapers
Culver Pictures: pp. 60–61
Francis Hammond: pp. 34, 59
International Stock:
  p. 2: © J. Contreras Chacel
  p. 10: © Dario Perla
  pp. 21, 99: © Al Clayton
  pp. 33, 116: © Stockman
  p. 83: © Dick Dickinson
Liaison International:
  p. 89, Back Cover: © Mark Green
  p. 102: © Marcel Ehrhard

Rick Mariani: Cover, p. 51
Sara Matthews: p. 14
Photofest: pp. 16–17, 104–105
Courtesy of Dom Pérignon: p. 13
Courtesy of Louis Roederer: pp. 7, 48, 66,
72, 94, 108, 113
Courtesy of Remi Krug: p. 22
Courtesy of Champagne Mumm: p. 37
Courtesy of Champagne Nicholas Feuillate:
pp. 64, 76
Courtesy of Perrier-Jouët: p. 90
Courtesy of Moët & Chandon: pp. 71, 86
Courtesy of Christie's London, King Street:
p. 119
Courtesy of Veuve Clicquot: p. 120

This book has been bound
using handcraft methods
and Smyth-sewn to
ensure durability.

The dust jacket and interior
were designed by
Terry Peterson.

The text, photographs, and art
were edited and compiled by
Amy Lyons.

Edited by Ann Berkhausen and
Mary McGuire Ruggiero.

The text was set in Cochin.